Cooking with Coconut Oil

50 Mouthwatering Coconut Oil Recipes

Marie Adams

Copyrights

All rights reserved © Marie Adams and The Cookbook Publisher. No part of this publication or the information in it may be quoted from or reproduced in any form by means such as printing, scanning, photocopying, or otherwise without prior written permission of the copyright holder.

Disclaimer and Terms of Use

Effort has been made to ensure that the information in this book is accurate and complete. However, the author and the publisher do not warrant the accuracy of the information, text, and graphics contained within the book due to the rapidly changing nature of science, research, known and unknown facts, and internet. The author and the publisher do not hold any responsibility for errors, omissions, or contrary interpretation of the subject matter herein. This book is presented solely for motivational and informational purposes only.

The recipes provided in this book are for informational purposes only and are not intended to provide dietary advice. A medical practitioner should be consulted before making any changes in diet. Additionally, recipe cooking times may require adjustment depending on age and quality of appliances. Readers are strongly urged to take all precautions to ensure ingredients are fully cooked in order to avoid the dangers of foodborne illnesses. The recipes and suggestions provided in this book are solely the opinion of the author. The author and publisher do not take any responsibility for any consequences that may result due to following the instructions provided in this book.

ISBN: 978-1533115973

Printed in the USA

Contents

Introduction 6
Benefits of Adding Coconut Oil to Your Diet 8
Five Tips When Cooking with Coconut Oil 10
Losing Weight with Coconut Oil 14
Breakfast Recipes 16
    Healthy Cranberry Breakfast Muffins 16
    Gluten-Free Pumpkin Pancakes 18
    Tropical Coconut Waffles 20
    Maple Cinnamon Coconut Granola 22
    Banana Coconut Green Smoothie 23
    Coconut Banana Bread 24
    Chicken and Turkey RecipesSimple 26
    Coconut Chicken Curry 26
    Home-Made Pesto Chicken Breasts 28
    Thai-Inspired Coconut Lime Chicken 30
    Grandma's Coconut Fried Chicken 32
    Sticky Sesame Chicken 34
    Coconut Roasted Whole Turkey 36
    All-American Turkey Burger 38
    Juicy Turkey Meatballs in Home-Made Tomato Sauce 40
    Pan-Fried Lemon Chicken 42
Beef and Veal Recipes 44
    Slow-Cooker Ground Beef Chili 44
    Beer Braised Short Ribs 46
    Beef and Broccoli Stir-Fry 48
    Spicy Thai Beef with Basil 50
    Hearty Home-Made Beef Stew 52
    Granny's Veal Meatloaf 54
    Italian Veal Chops 56
    Braised Veal Cheeks with Coconut Risotto 57
Pork and Lamb Recipes 60
    Pork Chops with Sweet Onion Jam 60
    Thai Pork Chops with Creamy Coconut Ginger Sauce 62

- Chinese Ginger Pork and Leek Stir-Fry 64
- Pineapple Sweet and Sour Pork 66
- Crock Pot Lamb Stew 68
- Pakistani Lamb Handi Curry 70
- Lamb Kofta with Tzatziki Sauce 72
- Rosemary and Garlic Lamb Chops 74

Vegetarian Recipes 76
- Sweet Potato and Chickpea Curry 76
- Coconut Butternut Squash Soup 78
- Roasted Cauliflower with Lentils Salad 80
- Kale and Brussels Sprouts Stir-Fry Noodles 82
- Fried Rice with Broccoli and Tofu 84
- Quinoa Tabbouleh Salad 86
- Spinach Sweet Potato Salad with Coconut Lime Dressing ...88
- Kale and Red Pepper Frittata 90
- Baked Sweet Potato Fries 92
- Coconut Hummus Dip or Dressing 93

Side Dish Recipes 94
- Honey-Coconut Glazed Carrots 94
- Zesty Coconut Rice with Cilantro 95
- Easy Garlic and Soy Stir-Fry Vegetables 96
- Roasted Garlic and Rosemary Potato Wedges 98
- Cauliflower Fried Rice 99
- Caramelized Onions and Mushroom Couscous 100

Dessert Recipes 102
- Coconut Oil Puffed Rice Treats 102
- Dairy-Free Coconut Chocolate Truffles 104
- Key Lime Pie 106
- Coconut Oil Chocolate Chip Cookies 108
- Fudgy Chocolate Coconut Brownie 110
- Moist Carrot Cake 112
- Coconut Glazed Donuts 114
- Rich Coconut Lemon Bars 116
- Chocolate Coconut Cupcakes 118
- No-bake Coconut Truffle Balls 120

Conclusion 122
Appendix - Cooking Conversion Charts 123

Introduction

The uses of the coconut fruit are fast becoming well known in the modern household. It is increasingly being picked up by the mainstream health community for its plethora of benefits. As a beauty product, it is known to be highly moisturizing with anti-bacterial properties, making it suitable for use in lotions, hair conditioners, mouthwashes, and lip balms. While its water, which is a clear liquid found in the center of young coconuts, is now touted as a hydrating drink that sportspeople can reach for to replace lost sugars and electrolytes. And in the kitchen, coconut oil is making a comeback.

Having once vilified it for its high saturated fat content, dieticians and nutritionists now consider coconut oil's saturated fats as its saving grace. About 84% of its calories come from saturated fat, as compared to 14% in olive oil and 63% in butter. And it is this exact property that helps coconut oil stay solid at room temperature, and extend its long shelf life.

Health authorities have long advised against eating a diet high in saturated fat, for it raises the level of the kind of cholesterol that increases the risk of developing heart diseases. Today, there is still little doubt that the saturated fats in butter, lard, sausages, and meat are bad for the body, but coconut oil has been shown to contain a different kind of saturated fat, containing medium-chain triglycerides (MCTs), which have a number of health-promoting properties we will further explore in our next section.

Health benefits aside, from a culinary point of view coconut oil is a versatile cooking oil that is naturally aromatic and adds a tropical punch to spice things up. Its ability to stand up to high heat also makes it suitable for a wide range of cooking methods from sautéing to roasting, and it can be used to make both savory and sweet food. It has also been well received by vegans, who do not eat any animal products, and paleo dieters, who eschew dairy. Both groups view coconut oil as a fantastic substitute for butter or margarine.

Also, please note that there is an appendix at the end of the book with cooking conversion tables to help you if needed.

Benefits of Adding Coconut Oil to Your Diet

Coconut oil is high in saturated fats, in particular medium-chain triglycerides (MCTs). MCTs are different from the saturated fats in butter, lard, and sausages, which are also known as long-chain triglycerides (LCT). This is because it is a shorter chain fatty acid that is more easily broken down and digested, and can be sent much quicker to the liver for energy production. Because energy can be generated faster, this also helps with increasing metabolism rates, allowing fats to be utilized rather than stored.

Additionally, a large portion of the MCT is made up of lauric acid, which is also a substance found in abundance in human breast milk. Because lauric acid in coconut oil is derived from plants, it is not paired with cholesterol as with the case of animal-derived fats. Therefore, coconut oil appears to be a healthier choice than other fat sources for it seems to help lower cholesterol levels rather than resulting in cholesterol build-up. In a 2007 study, researchers found that people who took MCT oil in place of corn oil had lower blood cholesterol at the end of the study. Other studies also show that lauric acid can increase 'good' HDL cholesterol and lower 'bad' LDL cholesterol.

Furthermore, virgin coconut oil also has anti-fungal and antioxidant properties. Studies have found that coconut oil helps improve the absorption of carotenoids, which produces an antioxidant effect which inhibits the oxidation of 'bad' LDL cholesterol. Consuming coconut oil has also been believed to help with treating yeast infections, with minimal side effects.

In spite of these health benefits, coconut oil, like any other oil, is inherently high in calories, and it should still be consumed moderately, particularly for those on a calorie-restricted diet.

Five Tips When Cooking with Coconut Oil

1. *There are two types of coconut oil*

There are refined and unrefined coconut oils. The refined version refers to coconut oil that has been industrially processed and bleached from dried coconut meat. During the process, high heat is also used to remove the oil's distinctive flavor and aroma. The end product is a neutral oil that would not overpower delicate food items and could be used in the same way as sunflower or rapeseed oil for sautéing and baking in general.

On the contrary, unrefined coconut oil, commonly known as virgin or pure coconut oil, retains the oil's natural flavor and aroma because it is extracted from fresh, rather than dried, coconut meat. No bleach or additives were used during the extraction, and it is also not exposed to the high heat that affects its original odor. This means that when cooking with unrefined coconut oil, the food will be infused with the 'coconutty' flavor and aroma.

2. *Coconut oil has different smoking points*

Knowing the smoking point of cooking fats is important because when heated past the smoke point, fats will start releasing free radicals and toxic fumes that will make food burn and give off an acrid flavor and aroma.

The higher the smoking point, the more cooking methods the fat can be used for.

Coconut oil has a medium smoking point that is similar to butter (350°F) but higher than extra virgin olive oil (325-375°F). Unfiltered coconut oil has a smoke point around 350°F, whereas refined coconut oil will withstand cooking temperatures up to around 450°F. This makes coconut oil a versatile cooking oil to work with. If you are looking to deep fry or sear steaks, use the refined version. If you are sautéing or simply looking to enhance the flavor profile of your food, then both oils work well, depending on your taste preferences.

3. Coconut oil is also great for baking

The high saturated fat content in coconut oil makes its composition very similar to butter and also resistant to oxidation at high temperatures. These reasons make coconut oil a healthier substitute for shortening, butter, margarine, or vegetable oil, and it makes the dish vegan as well!

To substitute coconut oil for butter in recipes, it is important to understand that coconut oil, unlike butter, is made up of mostly from fats, and this requires a recalibration in the amount of ingredient used. To do so, reduce the amount of fat needed by 25% when using coconut oil, and add a small amount of moisture to back to the recipe, because butter typically releases a small amount of moisture when baking. Adding a splash of liquid to recipes that use coconut oil will ensure that the baked product remains moist.

4. Coconut oil exists in a solid state at room temperature

Unlike most forms of cooking oil, coconut oil solidifies very quickly and can be rock hard during the winter months. The fastest way to melt coconut oil for a recipe would be to heat it in a saucepan over low heat. Once it reaches 76°F, it will naturally liquefy. Alternatively, keep your coconut oil at a warm spot in your kitchen, such as on the back of the stove or near the oven, so it will remain liquid most of the time.

If you are using it to bake, coconut oil will clump together very quickly when it mixes with cold ingredients such as milk and eggs. It is best to bring these refrigerated ingredients to room temperature before combining them with the oil, or simply, pop the coconut oil into the microwave for 20-30 seconds to liquefy it first.

5. Coconut oil is not only for cooking or baking

Coconut oil can also be added to both hot and cold drinks to enhance the flavor and health benefits. It might sound odd, but paleo adherents swear by a cup of 'bulletproof' coffee, or a mix of coffee, butter, and oil, every morning, for its purported effect of fuelling the body by helping caffeine slowly release into the body for a longer period of time. It also changes the texture of the drinks, making them smoother and creamier.

For cold beverages, the oil is best added to drinks with a thick consistency such as a smoothie or shake to prevent large clumps from forming. As for hot beverages, the oil is likely to float on the top of the water due to density differences. To mitigate the issue, try mixing the oil with dry ingredients such as hot chocolate mix or with honey before pouring the water.

Losing Weight with Coconut Oil

Coconut oil might be able encourage weight loss due to how the oil is structured as well as how the body processes the oil. In a 2009 study, women who had abdominal obesity were found to be able to lose more weight when they supplemented their diet with coconut oil rather than soy bean oil.

In terms of the oil's structure, although the coconut oil comprises a high level of saturated fats, most of them are MCTs. MCTs are able to dissolve in water more easily than olive or canola oil, which makes it easier for the body to access them for energy.

With shorter fatty chains, the liver is better able to digest MCTs than LCTs, which helps speed up and increase the body's energy levels. Instead of sending the fatty acid for storage, the faster processing speed also means that MCTs are instead being sent to the muscles to be used for energy, reducing the rate of heart-associated problems

Furthermore, the MCTs in coconut oil also help give the feeling of fullness, thus reducing food cravings. Weight loss is therefore achieved through the combination of better utilization of energy and decreasing food consumption. In a laboratory study, mice that were fed food containing MCTs gained less weight than their counterparts who were fed food containing LCTs.

Breakfast Recipes

Healthy Cranberry Breakfast Muffins

Servings: 16-18

Ingredients
2 ripe bananas, mashed
1 large egg
¼ cup coconut oil
1/3 cup milk
1/3 cup sugar
1 cup whole wheat flour
1 ¾ cups rolled oats
3 teaspoons baking powder
¼ cup walnuts, chopped
1-1½ cups fresh cranberries
Cinnamon

Preparation
1. Heat the oven to 375°F. Grease a muffin tin, or line it with paper liners.
2. Mash the bananas well before combining them with the egg, coconut oil, and milk.
3. Add the sugar, flour, rolled oats, baking powder, and a pinch of cinnamon. Mix just until incorporated. Gently fold in the walnuts and cranberries.
4. Pour the batter into the muffin cups until ¾ full, and bake for 20-25 minutes, or until a toothpick inserted in the center comes out clean.
5. Take the muffins out of the tin and cool on a wire rack.

Nutritional Facts (64 g per single serving)
Calories 187
Fats 6 g
Carbs 29 g
Protein 5 g
Sodium 12 mg

Gluten-Free Pumpkin Pancakes

Servings: 7

Ingredients
3 eggs
¼ cup pumpkin puree
3 tablespoons almond or coconut milk
1 tablespoon maple syrup
1 tablespoon coconut oil, melted, plus additional for greasing the pan
1 teaspoon vanilla extract
¼ cup coconut flour
½ teaspoon salt
¼ teaspoon baking soda
1 teaspoon cinnamon
Pinch of nutmeg

Preparation
1. In a medium bowl, beat the eggs lightly, and add the pumpkin puree, almond milk, maple syrup, coconut oil, and vanilla. Stir to combine.
2. In a large bowl, combine the coconut flour, salt, baking soda, cinnamon, and nutmeg.
3. Combine the wet ingredients into the dry mixture in 2 to 3 batches, each time stirring to combine. Do not overmix the batter, which will result in chewy rather than fluffy pancakes.
4. Heat a non-stick skillet on medium heat, and coat it with coconut oil.
5. Pour ¼ cup of batter on the skillet and wait until bubbles form and the edges look dry before flipping the pancake to cook on the other side.
6. Serve pancakes warm with maple syrup.

Nutritional Facts (50 g per single serving)
Calories 83
Fats 5 g
Carbs 6 g
Protein 4 g
Sodium 26 mg

Tropical Coconut Waffles

Servings: 6

Ingredients
1 ½ cups unsweetened coconut flakes
1 ½ cups all-purpose flour
½ cup cornstarch
1 teaspoon salt
1 teaspoon baking powder
½ teaspoon baking soda
2 large eggs
1 cup buttermilk
1 cup whole milk
2/3 cup coconut oil, melted
½ cup sugar
Non-stick cooking spray
Butter
Maple syrup
Pineapple, diced

Preparation
1. Heat a large skillet over medium, and toast the coconut flakes until golden brown.
2. In a large bowl, mix the flour, cornstarch, salt, baking powder, and baking soda.
3. In a separate bowl, whisk the eggs, buttermilk, milk, coconut oil, and sugar.
4. Combine the wet ingredients into the dry mixture, stirring just to combine. Add ½ of the toasted coconut. Do not overmix the batter, which will result in chewy rather than fluffy waffles.
5. Heat a waffle iron and coat it with non-stick spray. Cook the waffles until they are golden brown.

6. Serve the waffles warm with butter, maple syrup, pineapple chunks, and coconut flakes.

Nutritional Facts (219 g per single serving)
Calories 701
Fats 44 g
Carbs 68 g
Protein 11 g
Sodium 84 mg

Maple Cinnamon Coconut Granola

Makes: 7 cups of granola

Ingredients
3 cups large coconut flakes, unsweetened
1 cup fine coconut flakes, unsweetened
2 cups chopped nuts (pecan, almond, walnut)
1 cup pumpkin seeds
1 teaspoon sea salt
1 ½ teaspoons cinnamon
1 tablespoon vanilla extract
2 tablespoons coconut oil
⅓-½ cup maple syrup

Preparation
1. Preheat the oven to 300°F.
2. In a large bowl, mix all the ingredients thoroughly, and spread the mixture evenly on a 9x13 baking pan.
3. Bake for 35-40 minutes, taking it out to stir every 10 minutes. This will help prevent the granola from burning.
4. Take granola out of the oven and allow it to cool completely before transferring it to an airtight container.

Nutritional Facts (143 g per single serving)
Calories 793
Fats 69 g
Carbs 37 g
Protein 18 g
Sodium 31 mg

Banana Coconut Green Smoothie

Servings: 2

Ingredients:
2 frozen bananas
2 cups fresh spinach, washed
2 cups coconut water
2 teaspoons coconut oil
Cinnamon (optional)

Preparation:
1. Place all ingredients in the blender and blend until smooth.
2. Top the smoothie with cinnamon if desired.

Nutritional Facts (402 g per single serving)
Calories 279
Fats 14 g
Carbs 37 g
Protein 4 g
Sodium 277 mg

Coconut Banana Bread

Makes: 1 loaf

Ingredients
⅓ cup coconut oil, melted
½ cup honey or maple syrup
2 eggs
2 large bananas, mashed
¼ cup coconut milk
1 teaspoon vanilla extract
1 ¾ cups whole wheat flour
1 teaspoon baking soda
½ teaspoon salt
½ teaspoon ground cinnamon
½ cup chopped walnuts and coconut flakes, unsweetened

Preparation
1. Preheat the oven to 350°F, and grease a 9x5 loaf pan with coconut oil.
2. Using an electric hand mixer, whisk the coconut oil and honey before adding the eggs, bananas, milk, and vanilla. Combine until well blended.
3. In a small bowl, mix the flour, baking soda, salt, and cinnamon.
4. Add the dry ingredients to the wet ingredients in 3-4 small batches until just combined. Pour the batter into the loaf pan.
5. Bake for 40-50 minutes, or until a toothpick inserted in the center comes out clean.
6. Let the loaf cool on a wire rack before slicing it.

Nutritional Facts
Calories 4240
Fats 267 g
Carbs 403 g
Protein 112 g
Sodium 2565 mg

Chicken and Turkey RecipesSimple

Coconut Chicken Curry

Servings: 6

Ingredients
2 tablespoons coconut oil
3 tablespoons curry powder
1 large onion, diced
3 cloves garlic, minced
1 (14-ounce) can coconut milk
2 cups water
2 potatoes, cut into bite-sized chunks
1 teaspoon sugar
2 teaspoons salt
4 boneless skinless chicken thighs, cut into bite-sized chunks

Preparation
1. Heat the coconut oil in a large skillet over medium heat.
2. Fry the diced onion for 2-3 minutes. Add the curry powder and give it a good stir. When it is fragrant, add the garlic.
3. Pour in the coconut milk and water, and bring the liquid to a boil. To prevent the coconut milk from curdling, avoid using high heat and stir constantly.
4. Add the potato chunks, together with the salt and sugar. Cover the skillet and simmer on low heat for 10-15 minutes, or until the potato is cooked

5. Throw in the chicken chunks and allow everything to cook for another 10-15 minutes, until the chicken is cooked through and potatoes are fork tender.
6. Adjust the seasonings to taste.

Nutritional Facts (360 g per single serving)
Calories 422
Fats 28 g
Carbs 22 g
Protein 24 g
Sodium 889 mg

Home-Made Pesto Chicken Breasts

Servings: 4

Ingredients
¼ cup pine nuts
1 cup basil
2 tablespoons olive oil
2 tablespoons coconut oil, melted
3 cloves garlic, peeled
¼ cup Parmesan cheese, grated
4 skinless chicken breasts
1 tomato, diced
1 cup mozzarella cheese, grated
Salt and pepper

Preparation
1. Heat a small frying pan over low heat and toast the pine nuts until brown.
2. Place the nuts, basil, olive oil, coconut oil, garlic, and Parmesan cheese into a food processor. Blend until a smooth paste is formed.
3. Preheat the oven to 350°F. Line a baking pan with parchment paper.
4. Cover the chicken breasts on both sides with the pesto. Season with salt and pepper.
5. Arrange the chicken breasts on the pan and bake for 30 minutes.
6. Remove the chicken from the oven and top it off with mozzarella cheese and diced tomato.
7. Bake for another 20 minutes, or until the internal temperature reaches 165°F.

Nutritional Facts (367 g per single serving)
Calories 624
Fats 34 g
Carbs 5 g
Protein 71 g
Sodium 414 mg

Thai-Inspired Coconut Lime Chicken

Servings: 4

Ingredients
1-inch piece of fresh ginger, peeled and roughly chopped
1 tablespoon fish sauce, or soy sauce
1 cup coconut milk
2 cloves garlic, peeled
¼ cup fresh cilantro
2 tablespoons brown sugar
Zest of 2 limes
4 chicken thighs
2 tablespoons coconut oil
Salt and pepper

Preparation
1. Place the ginger, fish sauce (or soy sauce), coconut milk, garlic, cilantro, sugar and lime zest in a food processor. Blend until smooth.
2. Combine the marinade with the chicken thighs in a plastic storage bag. Refrigerate for at least 30 minutes, or overnight.
3. Pre-heat the oven to 350°F.
4. Heat an oven-safe, medium-sized skillet over medium heat. Melt the coconut oil.
5. Pan-fry both sides of the marinated chicken until golden brown, about 5-8 minutes on each side.
6. Place the skillet inside the oven for another 25-30 minutes, or until the chicken is thoroughly cooked.

Nutritional Facts (296 g per single serving)
Calories 664
Fats 53 g
Carbs 15 g
Protein 34 g
Sodium 475 mg

Grandma's Coconut Fried Chicken

Servings: 4-6

Ingredients
1 (2-3 pound) chicken, cut into 8 pieces
Coconut oil for frying (enough to cover the chicken pieces in the saucepan)
Dipping sauce for serving

Marinade
4 cups coconut milk
1 teaspoon (or more) hot sauce
1 teaspoon salt
1 teaspoon black pepper

Dredging Mixture
1 teaspoon garlic powder
1 teaspoon cayenne pepper (or more if you like it spicier)
1 teaspoon salt
1 teaspoon black pepper
1 teaspoon cumin
1 teaspoon dry thyme
1 teaspoon baking powder
2 ½ cups all-purpose flour

Preparation
1. In a large mixing bowl, whisk together the coconut milk, hot sauce, salt, and black pepper. Add the chicken pieces. The coconut milk mixture should cover the chicken. Using your hands, make sure the chicken pieces are well covered in coconut milk. Refrigerate for at least 3 hours, or up to 12 hours.

2. Remove the chicken from the refrigerator at least 1 hour before cooking to bring it up to room temperature.
3. In a large, deep pot, heat the coconut oil to 350°F. You can also use a deep cast iron skillet, filled to the ¾ mark with the oil.
4. Prepare the dredging mixture in a shallow bowl by adding all the ingredients and mixing well.
5. Remove the chicken pieces from the coconut milk mixture and dredge them in the flour one piece at a time. Shake gently to remove any excess flour. Carefully lower each piece into the hot oil with a slotted spoon.
6. Do not crowd all the chicken pieces together; cook half the chicken at a time until crispy and brown, about 15 minutes, turning halfway. Once cooked, remove the chicken pieces with a slotted spoon and drain them on a paper towels.
7. To check the doneness of the chicken, poke the chicken with a fork on the thickest part of the chicken to make sure the juices run clear, or that the internal temperature reads at least 165°F on an instant read meat thermometer when inserted in the thickest part of the chicken piece without touching a bone.
8. Enjoy while hot, with the dipping sauce of your choice!

Nutritional Facts (354 g per single serving)
Calories 858
Fats 59 g
Carbs 49 g
Protein 35 g
Sodium 918 mg

Sticky Sesame Chicken

Servings: 4

Ingredients
2/3 cup water
½ cup honey
3 tablespoons soy sauce
2 teaspoons sesame oil
1 teaspoon white vinegar
1 garlic clove, finely minced
1 teaspoon ginger, grated
Salt
White pepper
1 cup + 1 ½ tablespoons cornstarch, divided
1 ½ tablespoons cold water
Coconut oil, for frying
1 teaspoon baking powder
2 eggs
1 ½ pounds chicken breast, cut into bite-sized pieces
1 tablespoon sesame seeds
Scallions, chopped (optional for garnish)

Preparation
1. In a small saucepan, combine the water, honey, soy sauce, sesame oil, vinegar, garlic, ginger, salt and pepper. Bring the liquid to a boil.
2. Prepare a slurry by mixing 1 ½ tablespoons of cornstarch with 1 ½ tablespoons of cold water until well combined.
3. Drizzle the slurry into the boiling honey mixture while stirring constantly. The mixture will thicken up in 3-5 minutes. Remove it from the heat.

4. In a large deep pot, heat the coconut oil to 350°F. You can also use a deep cast iron skillet, filled to the ¾ mark with oil.
5. Prepare 2 shallow dishes. Whisk the eggs in one, and combine 1 cup of cornstarch with the baking powder in the other.
6. Dredge the chicken pieces first into the egg and then into the cornstarch mixture, coating each piece evenly.
7. Cook half the chicken for about 5-7 minutes until golden brown, turning it once halfway through.
8. Once cooked, remove the chicken pieces with a slotted spoon and drain on a paper towel.
9. Toss the fried chicken pieces with the sauce, and coat generously with sesame seeds. Finish it off with scallions, if desired.

Nutritional Facts (295 g per single serving)
Calories 448
Fats 11 g
Carbs 49 g
Protein 38 g
Sodium 335 mg

Coconut Roasted Whole Turkey

Servings: 10-14

Ingredients
1 large turkey (about 13 pounds) with neck
2 lemons, zested and halved
1 onion, cut into rings
1 cups white wine
4 cups chicken broth
2 cloves garlic, minced
¼ cup flat-leaf parsley, minced
2 teaspoons thyme, minced
½ cup coconut oil
Salt and white pepper

Preparation
1. If the turkey is frozen, make sure it is completely thawed by keeping it in the refrigerator for a day or two. Remove the neck and gizzards from the cavity.
2. When you are ready to cook the bird, take it out of the fridge and leave it to sit for at least 30 minutes to let it come to room temperature.
3. Preheat the oven to 400°F and place the rack at the lowest point in the oven. Set the roasting rack in the roasting pan.
4. Rinse and pat the turkey dry. Place the lemon halves in the cavity, and use a piece of kitchen twine to truss the bird.
5. Place the turkey neck, onion, wine, and broth in the roasting pan to make drippings for gravy.
6. In a mixing bowl, combine the garlic, lemon zest, parsley, thyme, and coconut oil to form a paste.

Rub the turkey with the paste generously and season with salt and pepper.
7. Transfer the turkey onto the roasting rack and into the oven.
8. Cook the turkey at 400°F for 30 minutes, then turn the oven down to 350°F for another 2 hours and 15 minutes. Take the meat out of the oven every 30 mins to baste it with the drippings collected at the bottom of the pan.
9. The turkey is done when the skin is golden brown and a meat thermometer reads 160°F when stuck into the thigh. If the turkey skin is browning too quickly before the meat is cooked, place aluminum foil over it to form a tent.
10. Remove the turkey from the oven and let it rest for at least 30 minutes before carving.

Nutritional Facts (501 g per single serving)
Calories 730
Fats 30 g
Carbs 3 g
Protein 84 g
Sodium 717 mg

All-American Turkey Burger

Servings: 4

Ingredients

1 ½ pounds ground turkey
½ cup mozzarella cheese, grated
¼ cup dried breadcrumbs
1 tablespoon Worcestershire sauce
¼ cup Dijon mustard
1 garlic clove, finely minced
¼ cup onion, finely minced
2 tablespoons coconut oil, plus some more for greasing
¼ teaspoon salt
¼ teaspoon black pepper
4 soft rolls
4 lettuce leaves
2 tomatoes, sliced
Cheese slice of your choice
Barbecue sauce

Preparation

1. In a medium bowl, combine the ground turkey, mozzarella, breadcrumbs, Worcestershire sauce, mustard, garlic, onion, coconut oil, salt and pepper, until well blended.
2. Form the mixture into four patties that are 1 inch thick.
3. Prepare the grate by brushing it with coconut oil. Turn heat to high.
4. Cook the patties by placing it first on the hottest part of the grill. Brown the meat for 1 to 2 minutes on each side then shift it to the cooler side (or lower the heat) and continue grilling for about 20 minutes, or until completely cooked through.

5. Serve the patties on soft bread rolls with lettuce, tomatoes, cheese, and a generous dollop of barbecue sauce

Nutritional Facts (352 g per single serving)
Calories 506
Fats 25 g
Carbs 24 g
Protein 47 g
Sodium 569 mg

Juicy Turkey Meatballs in Home-Made Tomato Sauce

Servings: 5

Ingredients
For meatballs:
1 ¾ pounds ground turkey
1 tablespoon coconut oil
1 onion, finely diced
1 clove garlic, finely minced
2 tablespoons parsley, chopped
2 eggs
Salt and black pepper

For sauce:
2 tablespoons coconut oil
1 onion, diced
2 (14.5-ounce) cans diced tomatoes
1 clove garlic, minced
1 teaspoon dried thyme
1 teaspoon dried oregano
1 teaspoon dried basil
Salt

Preparation
1. Preheat the oven to 375°F.
2. In a medium bowl, combine all the meatball ingredients and season generously with salt and pepper. Roll the meatballs into golf ball-sized pieces, and place them in a roasting pan.
3. To make the sauce, heat the coconut oil in a medium-sized skillet on medium heat.
4. Add the onions and cook until translucent.

5. Add the tomatoes, garlic, thyme, oregano, and basil, and season with salt to taste. Cook for about 10 minutes.
6. Pour the sauce over the meatballs, and bake for 25-35 minutes or until the meatballs are cooked through.

Nutritional Facts (423 g per single serving)
Calories 419
Fats 23 g
Carbs 19 g
Protein 37 g
Sodium 439 mg

Pan-Fried Lemon Chicken

Servings: 1

Ingredients
1 chicken breast
1 lemon, zest and juice
1-2 teaspoons coconut oil, melted
¼ teaspoon sea salt
⅛ teaspoon black pepper

Preparation
1. Place the chicken breast in between two pieces of parchment, or inside a plastic bag. Use a meat tenderizer to pound the chicken breast to an even thickness, starting from the thickest part first.
2. Rub the meat thoroughly with lemon juice and zest, coconut oil, salt, and pepper. Allow it to marinate for at least 30 minutes.
3. Heat a skillet over medium heat and melt the coconut oil.
4. Cook the chicken for about 5 minutes on each side, or until the internal temperature reaches 165°F.

Nutritional Facts (79 g per single serving)
Calories 146
Fats 9 g
Carbs 1 g
Protein 15 g
Sodium 176 mg

Beef and Veal Recipes

Slow-Cooker Ground Beef Chili

Servings: 6

Ingredients
1 tablespoon coconut oil, melted
1 onion, diced
4 cloves garlic, minced
1 green bell pepper, chopped
1 ½ pounds ground beef
1 butternut squash, cut into chunks
2 (14.5-ounce) cans diced tomatoes
1 (14.5-ounce) kidney beans
3 tablespoons chili powder
Salt and pepper

Preparation
1. Heat the coconut oil in a medium skillet over medium-high heat.
2. Add the onion and fry until translucent before adding the garlic, bell pepper, and ground beef.
3. Crumble the ground beef while stirring the mixture for about 8-10 minutes.
4. Transfer the meat mixture into a 4-6 quart slow cooker. Add the squash, tomatoes, kidney beans, and chili powder. Season with salt and pepper to taste.
5. Cover and cook on low for 4-6 hours, or on high for 2-3 hours.

Nutritional Facts (523 g per single serving)
Calories 428
Fats 19 g
Carbs 45 g
Protein 24 g
Sodium 495 mg

Beer Braised Short Ribs

Servings: 4

Ingredients
3 pounds short ribs,
2 tablespoons coconut oil, melted
Salt and pepper
1 onion, sliced
4 cloves garlic, minced
3 cups dark beer, such as stout
2 to 4 sprigs fresh herbs, such as rosemary or thyme

Preparation
1. Preheat the oven to 325°F.
2. Coat the ribs with coconut oil and season them with salt and pepper.
3. Heat a deep and wide oven-safe sauté pan over medium-high heat. Add the short ribs to the pan and arrange them in a single layer. Using a pair of tongs, sear each side for a few minutes, or until they are deep brown in color.
4. Turn the heat down to medium, and add the onion and garlic. Allow the onion to sweat for about 5 minutes.
5. Pour the stout into the pot and bring it to a simmer.
6. Place the herb sprigs on top of the ribs. Cover the pan with a lid and place it into the oven to cook for 2-2 ½ hours, or until the meat becomes fork tender.
7. Once done, take the meat out of the oven and let it rest in the covered pan for at least 20 minutes before serving.

Nutritional Facts (557 g per single serving)
Calories 759
Fats 43 g
Carbs 12 g
Protein 68 g
Sodium 290 mg

Beef and Broccoli Stir-Fry

Servings: 4

Ingredients
2 tablespoons coconut oil
1 pound flank steak, boneless sirloin or skirt steak, cut into ½ inch strips
½ cup soy sauce
3 cloves garlic, minced
2 tablespoons honey
1 teaspoon fresh ginger, grated
2 tablespoons sesame oil
1 pinch red pepper flakes
2 tablespoons cornstarch
2 tablespoons water
1 head broccoli, cut into bite-sized florets

Preparation
1. In a medium bowl, whisk together the soy sauce, garlic, honey, ginger, sesame oil, and red pepper flakes.
2. Add the beef strips, coat the meat well with the sauce and allow it to marinate for 20 minutes.
3. Heat 1 tablespoon of the coconut oil in a large saute pan over high heat. Cook the beef for 4 minutes and remove it to a clean bowl. Keep the marinade.
4. While the meat is cooking, whisk the cornstarch with water and set it aside.
5. Heat another tablespoon of coconut oil and fry the broccoli for 2 minutes before adding the beef back into the pan.
6. Pour the remaining sauce into the pan, together with the cornstarch mixture.

7. Mix everything thoroughly and cook until the sauce bubbles and thickens, about 2 minutes.

Nutritional Facts (211 g per single serving)
Calories 431
Fats 28 g
Carbs 19 g
Protein 26 g
Sodium 2050 mg

Spicy Thai Beef with Basil

Servings: 4

Ingredients
2 tablespoons coconut oil
5 cloves garlic, chopped
1 shallot, chopped
2 bird's eye chilies, remove seeds for less heat
1 pound ground beef
2 tablespoons soy sauce
2 tablespoons dark soy sauce
1 tablespoon fish sauce
2 teaspoons sugar
2 tablespoons lime juice
2 cups fresh basil leaves
Pepper

Preparation
1. Heat the coconut oil in a wok or large skillet over medium-high heat. Cook the garlic, shallot, and chili in the oil for 1 minute.
2. Cook the beef until brown, about 5-7 minutes. Use a wooden spoon to break the meat up into smaller pieces. Season it generously with pepper.
3. Add the soy sauces, fish sauce, sugar, and lime juice. Mix well and cook for 2 minutes before turning the heat off.
4. Mix in the basil. Using the residual heat, allow the basil to wilt for 1-2 minutes before serving.

Nutritional Facts (159 g per single serving)
Calories 372
Fats 26 g
Carbs 14 g
Protein 21 g
Sodium 680 mg

Hearty Home-Made Beef Stew

Servings: 6

Ingredients
2 tablespoons coconut oil
2 pounds stewing beef
1 onion, sliced
4 cups water
1 teaspoon Worcestershire sauce
1 teaspoon salt
1 teaspoon sugar
½ teaspoon black pepper
½ teaspoon paprika
3 carrots, sliced
6 red potatoes, diced
1/3 cup tomato paste
4 teaspoons beef bouillon granules

Preparation
1. Heat the coconut oil in a large, deep pot over medium heat.
2. Cook the beef cubes until brown, about 10 minutes. Add the onion and allow it to soften for 2-3 minutes.
3. Add the water, Worcestershire sauce, salt, sugar, pepper, and paprika. Cover the pot and allow it to simmer on medium-low heat for an hour.
4. Stir in the carrots, potatoes, tomato paste, and beef granules before covering the pot with a lid and allowing it to simmer for another 45 mins, or until the potato becomes fork tender.

Nutritional Facts (539 g per single serving)
Calories 413
Fats 12 g
Carbs 40 g
Protein 37 g
Sodium 820 mg

Granny's Veal Meatloaf

Servings: 4

Ingredients
1 tablespoon coconut oil, plus some for greasing
1 onion, diced
1 pound ground veal
1 pound ground beef
1/3 cup sour cream
1 tablespoon Worcestershire sauce
½ cup Italian breadcrumbs
2 tablespoons of parsley, chopped
1 teaspoon dried thyme
1 teaspoon salt
1 teaspoon black pepper
2 eggs
4 slices bacon
3-4 tablespoons of barbecue sauce

Preparation
1. Preheat the oven to 375°F. Grease a 9x5 loaf pan with some of the coconut oil.
2. Heat the remaining coconut oil in a medium skillet over medium heat. Saute the onion until translucent. Remove it from the heat and let it cool.
3. In a large mixing bowl, combine the cooled onion, veal, beef, sour cream, Worcestershire sauce, breadcrumbs, parsley, thyme, salt, and pepper. Give it a mix before cracking in the eggs.
4. Combine the mixture well before pressing it into the loaf pan.
5. Bake for 30 minutes, then remove it from oven to drain the fat.

6. Place the bacon strips lengthwise across the meatloaf and return it to the oven for another 15 minutes.
7. Remove it from the oven once more to drain the fat. Generously apply the barbecue sauce all over the meatloaf before putting back into the oven for the last 15-20 minutes.
8. Once cooked through, take it out of the oven and let it rest for 5-10 minutes before serving.

Nutritional Facts (362 g per single serving)
Calories 793
Fats 55 g
Carbs 20 g
Protein 50 g
Sodium 782 mg

Italian Veal Chops

Servings: 4

Ingredients
4 veal chops
1 tablespoon coconut oil
½ teaspoon salt
¼ teaspoon black pepper
2 teaspoons oregano
2 cloves garlic, minced
2 (14.5-ounces) cans diced tomatoes
2 tablespoons parsley, chopped

Preparation
1. Heat the coconut oil in a large skillet over high heat.
2. Season the veal chops with salt, pepper, and oregano.
3. When the oil is shimmering, add the veal chops and brown on both sides.
4. Bring the heat down to medium-low, and cook the garlic until browned.
5. Reduce the heat further to low. Throw in the tomatoes and parsley, cover, and simmer for about 2 hours, or until the veal is cooked through.

Nutritional Facts (658 g per single serving)
Calories 763
Fats 38 g
Carbs 15 g
Protein 88 g
Sodium 1074 mg

Braised Veal Cheeks with Coconut Risotto

Servings: 4

Ingredients
For veal:
4 veal cheeks
Salt and pepper
2 tablespoons coconut oil
1 cup red wine
1 onion, diced
2 celery stalks, diced
1 carrot, diced
1 teaspoon fresh rosemary, chopped
1 teaspoon fresh sage, chopped
1 teaspoon fresh thyme, chopped
2 bay leaves
2 cloves garlic, minced
2 tablespoons tomato paste
2 cups beef stock
4 cups of chicken stock

For coconut risotto:
1 tablespoon coconut oil
1 cup short-grain rice, such as Arborio
1 cup dry white wine
1-2 cups hot water
1 (14 ounce) can coconut milk
Salt to taste

Preparation
1. Preheat the oven to 320°F.
2. Season the veal cheeks generously with salt and black pepper.
3. Heat 1 tablespoon of coconut oil in a large, deep, oven-safe skillet over high heat. Add the veal and cook for 4 minutes on each side, until browned all over. Remove from the heat.
4. Pour the red wine into the same skillet, and simmer on high heat until the liquid is reduced by half. Pour it into a clean dish and set it aside.
5. Melt the other tablespoon of coconut oil in the skillet. Add the onion, celery, and carrot, and saute for 4 minutes until softened, before throwing in the rosemary, sage, thyme, bay leaves, garlic, and tomato paste.
6. Return the veal to the pot, together with the reduced wine, beef stock, and chicken stock. Cover the skillet with a lid and bake for 4 ½ hours, or until the veal is tender.
7. During the final 20 minutes of cooking the veal, prepare the risotto. Heat the coconut oil in a medium-sized skillet over medium-high heat.
8. Add the rice and cook for 2 -3 minutes, until it is shiny and sizzling.
9. Pour in the white wine and cook until most of the liquid is absorbed. Add the hot water and stir the rice until most of the liquid is absorbed.
10. Add half of the coconut milk. Simmer and stir until most of the liquid is gone, then add the other half of the coconut milk.
11. Check whether the rice is tender. If it isn't, add an additional ½ cup of water and repeat the process.
12. Serve slices of the melt-in-your-mouth veal cheeks on top of the coconut risotto.

Nutritional Facts *(792 g per single serving)*
Calories 1265
Fats 46 g
Carbs 165 g
Protein 30 g
Sodium 882 mg

Pork and Lamb Recipes

Pork Chops with Sweet Onion Jam

Servings: 4

Ingredients
For the sweet onion jam:
3 large onions, peeled and thinly sliced
½ cup coconut oil
1 tablespoon fresh rosemary, chopped
1 tablespoon fresh thyme, chopped
2 tablespoons balsamic vinegar
2 tablespoons sugar

For the pork chops:
4 pork chops
1 tablespoon coconut oil
2 cloves garlic, minced
1 tablespoon fresh rosemary, chopped
1 tablespoon fresh thyme, chopped
1 teaspoon salt
1 teaspoon pepper
¼ cup flat-leaf parsley, chopped, for garnish

Preparation
1. Heat the coconut oil in a medium-sized skillet over medium heat. Add the onions and cook until translucent, about 15 minutes.
2. Reduce the heat to low and add the rosemary, thyme, balsamic vinegar, and sugar. Cover the pot and allow it to cook for 2 hours, stirring every 30 minutes to scrape up the caramelized bits on the bottom.

3. Once the onions reach a soft, jam-like consistency, remove them from the heat and set them aside.
4. Meanwhile, prepare the pork chops. In a small bowl, combine the garlic, rosemary, thyme, salt, and pepper, and rub the mixture onto both sides of the chops. Place the marinated meat in a clean bowl, cover it with plastic wrap, and keep it in the refrigerator.
5. Bring the pork chops out of the fridge to come to room temperature 30 minutes before the onion jam is done.
6. Heat a grill pan over medium-high heat. Brush it grill lightly with the coconut oil.
7. Place the chops on the grill, and cook until the surface releases from the grill, about 4-7 minutes on each side.
8. Serve immediately with the sweet onion jam, and garnish with some chopped parsley.

Nutritional Facts (332 g per single serving)
Calories 679
Fats 48 g
Carbs 16 g
Protein 42 g
Sodium 1280 mg

Thai Pork Chops with Creamy Coconut Ginger Sauce

Servings: 4

Ingredients

For the coconut ginger sauce:
1 (14-ounce) can coconut milk
1 teaspoon soy sauce
1 teaspoon sugar
1 teaspoon Thai chili sauce
1 tablespoon fish sauce
1 tablespoon lime juice

For the pork chops:
4 pork chops
2 tablespoons coconut oil, divided
½ onion, minced
1 red bell pepper, sliced
2 tomatoes, cut into wedges
1 tablespoon ginger, grated
2 cloves garlic, minced
Salt and pepper

Preparation
1. Whisk all the sauce ingredients together in a medium mixing bowl.
2. Heat 1 tablespoon of coconut oil in a large skillet over high heat. Meanwhile Season the pork chops generously with salt and pepper on both sides.
3. Once the skillet becomes very hot, sear the meat on both sides, about 2 minutes each, and set them aside.

4. Lower the heat to medium. Add the remaining 1 tablespoon of the coconut oil to the skillet. Cook the onion, pepper, and tomatoes for a minute before adding the ginger and garlic.
5. Reduce the heat to medium. Pour the coconut milk mixture into the pan and bring the sauce to a simmer, stirring constantly.
6. Add the pork chops to the sauce and cook until the sauce thickens and the meat is no longer pink in the middle.
7. Plate the pork chops with some of the sauce and mixed vegetables for a delicious and filling meal.

Nutritional Facts (438 g per single serving)
Calories 631
Fats 46 g
Carbs 12 g
Protein 45 g
Sodium 743 mg

Chinese Ginger Pork and Leek Stir-Fry

Servings: 2

Ingredients
10 ounces pork butt, cut into 2-inch strips
2 cloves garlic, minced, divided
1 leek, white and pale green parts, sliced diagonally ¼-inch thick
2 tablespoons coconut oil
1 teaspoon sesame oil
1 teaspoon dark soy sauce
½ teaspoon cornstarch
¼ teaspoon sugar

Preparation
1. In a medium bowl, whisk the sesame oil, soy sauce, cornstarch, sugar, and half the garlic. Add the pork and combine well. Let it marinate for at least 15 minutes
2. Heat 1 tablespoon of coconut oil in a large skillet over high heat.
3. Once the skillet becomes very hot, add the leeks and cook until fragrant, about 1 minute. Set them aside.
4. Add the remaining 1 tablespoon of coconut oil to the skillet. Cook the pork strips and garlic until the meat is browned, about 2 minutes.
5. Throw the leeks back into the pot, giving everything a good toss for another minute.
6. Serve piping hot.

Nutritional Facts (201 g per single serving)
Calories 378
Fats 27 g
Carbs 7 g
Protein 26 g
Sodium 301 mg

Pineapple Sweet and Sour Pork

Servings: 2-4

Ingredients
For the meat:
1 pound boneless pork loin, cut into 1-inch pieces
2 large eggs
¼ cup cornstarch
¼ cup all-purpose flour
1 tablespoon minced garlic
1 bell pepper, cut into bite-sized pieces
1 cup pineapple chunks, fresh or canned
1 tomato, chopped
1 tablespoon coconut oil, plus more for frying
Sesame seeds, for garnish

For the sauce:
3 tablespoons water
2 tablespoons ketchup
2 tablespoons pineapple juice, fresh or canned
1 ½ tablespoons cider vinegar
1 tablespoon Worcestershire sauce
1 tablespoon soy sauce
2 tablespoons sugar

Preparation
1. In a medium bowl, whisk together the eggs, cornstarch, and flour. Add the pork pieces and combine well.
2. Using a large, deep pot, heat enough coconut oil to submerge the meat pieces until it reaches 350°F.

3. Drop the pork into the oil in 2 or 3 batches, making sure to avoid overcrowding the meat. Fry until golden brown, 4 to 5 minutes for each batch.
4. Using a slotted spoon, remove the pork from the oil and drain off the excess oil on a plate lined with paper towels. Repeat the process until all the pork is cooked.
5. Whisk together all the sauce ingredients in a medium bowl.
6. Heat 1 tablespoon of coconut oil in a large skillet over medium-high heat. Add the garlic and bell pepper, and fry until aromatic.
7. Throw in the pineapple and tomato, and mix in the sauce. Simmer for 2 minutes to heat everything through and for the sauce to thicken slightly.
8. Add the pork and coat the meat generously with the sauce
9. Transfer it to a plate and garnish it with sesame seeds. Serve immediately.

Nutritional Facts (294 g per single serving)
Calories 365
Fats 11 g
Carbs 46 g
Protein 30 g
Sodium 520 mg

Crock Pot Lamb Stew

Servings: 4-6

Ingredients
2 ½ pounds boneless lamb stewing meat, cut up into ½-inch cubes
2 tablespoons coconut oil
¼ cup all-purpose flour
2 teaspoons salt
1 teaspoon sugar
½ teaspoon dried thyme
¼ teaspoon pepper
¼ teaspoon garlic powder
14 ounces beef broth, or water
3 large carrots, peeled and cut into bite-sized chunks
3 potatoes, peeled and cut into bite-sized chunks
1 onion, sliced
10 ounces frozen peas

Preparation
1. In a large bowl, toss the lamb cubes with the flour, salt, sugar, thyme, pepper, and garlic powder.
2. Heat the coconut oil in a medium skillet over medium-high heat. Add the lamb cubes.
3. Sear the meat for 3-4 minutes, until nicely browned, before transferring it into the crock pot.
4. Add the beef broth, carrots, potatoes and onion to the pot. Cover the pot and cook on low for 10 hours.
5. In the last 30 minutes before serving, add the peas.

Nutritional Facts (477 g per single serving)
Calories 460
Fats 15 g
Carbs 35 g
Protein 45 g
Sodium 1134 mg

Pakistani Lamb Handi Curry

Servings: 4-6

Ingredients
2 ½ pounds boneless lamb leg, cut up into cubes
4 tablespoons coconut oil
6 onions, chopped
2 tablespoons ginger, peeled and minced
2 tablespoons garlic paste
1 tablespoon cumin seeds
1 tablespoon coriander seeds
1 teaspoon mace
½ teaspoon red chili powder
3 green cardamom pods
2 whole cinnamon sticks
5 tomatoes, cut into wedges
4 cups water
3 bay leaves
2 cups Greek yogurt
1 teaspoon cornstarch
Salt

Preparation
1. In a large, deep skillet, heat the coconut oil over medium-high heat. Sauté the onions until translucent, about 10 minutes, then add the ginger and garlic.
2. Add the cumin, coriander, mace, chili, cardamom, and cinnamon to the skillet and cook until fragrant. Toss in the tomatoes and cook for about 10-15 minutes, stirring to break the tomatoes up so they become soft and mushy.
3. Cook the lamb in the tomato spice mixture for another 10-15 minutes.

4. Reduce the heat to low. Add the water and bay leaves. Cover with the lid and simmer for 30 minutes, or until the lamb becomes tender.
5. Whisk the cornstarch with the Greek yogurt.
6. Increase the heat to medium, and add the yogurt into the curry. Keep stirring the curry to prevent the yogurt from separating.
7. Cook until the gravy thickens.

Nutritional Facts (668 g per single serving)
Calories 721
Fats 52 g
Carbs 19 g
Protein 43 g
Sodium 176 mg

Lamb Kofta with Tzatziki Sauce

Servings: 4

Ingredients
For the tzatziki sauce:
½ cucumber, halved and seeded
½ teaspoon salt
1 cups plain full-fat Greek yogurt
1 clove garlic, finely minced
1 tablespoon extra virgin olive oil
1 tablespoon lemon juice
1 tablespoon fresh dill, minced

For the kofta:
1 ½ pounds ground lamb
2 tablespoons coconut oil, plus 1 tablespoon for grilling
1 onion, finely chopped
2 cloves garlic, crushed
1 tablespoon ground coriander
1 tablespoon ground cumin
½ tablespoon ground cinnamon
½ tablespoon ground allspice
¼ tablespoon cayenne pepper
¼ tablespoon ground ginger
1 cup flat-leaf parsley, roughly chopped
Salt and pepper

Preparation
1. To make the sauce, grate the cucumber and transfer it to a fine-mesh sieve. Sprinkle the salt over it and allow to sit in the sieve for at least an hour.
2. Using your hands, wring out as much water as possible from the cucumber.

3. Add the cucumber, garlic, olive oil, lemon juice, and dill to the yogurt. Give it a good mix and refrigerate it for at least an hour.
4. Heat the coconut oil in a large skillet over medium-high heat. Saute the onion and garlic until softened.
5. Add the coriander, cumin, cinnamon, allspice, cayenne, and ginger and fry until fragrant.
6. In a large mixing bowl, combine the lamb, the onion and spice mixture, and parsley. Season it generously with salt and pepper. Mix well.
7. Spoon out a dollop of the meat paste, and wrap it around a wooden skewer. This recipe should make 12 sticks. Refrigerate the kofta for at least an hour before cooking.
8. Heat a griddle pan over high heat. Once sizzling hot, place the skewer sticks on the pan and brush them with melted coconut oil. Allow the lamb to turn dark brown, grilling it for at least 3 minutes on each side.
9. Serve them warm with tzatziki sauce.

Nutritional Facts (433 g per single serving)
Calories 828
Fats 66 g
Carbs 11 g
Protein 46 g
Sodium 465 mg

Rosemary and Garlic Lamb Chops

Servings: 4

Ingredients
5 cloves garlic
3 tablespoons coconut oil, melted
2 ½ teaspoons fresh rosemary
2 teaspoons salt
1 teaspoon black pepper
12 lamb rib chops (2 ½ ounces each)

Preparation
1. In a food processor, make a paste from the garlic, coconut oil, rosemary, salt, and pepper.
2. Rub the rosemary paste all over the lamb chops, and allow them to marinate for at least 30 minutes or up to 8 hours in the refrigerator.
3. Heat a large skillet over medium-high heat and add the lamb. Cook for 3 minutes on each side to achieve medium-rare doneness.
4. Remove the lamb from the skillet and let it rest for 5 minutes before digging in.

Nutritional Facts (206 g per single serving)
Calories 545
Fats 42 g
Carbs 1 g
Protein 40 g
Sodium 1294 mg

Vegetarian Recipes

Sweet Potato and Chickpea Curry

Servings: 4

Ingredients
1 tablespoon coconut oil
1 tablespoon cumin seeds
1 onion, finely sliced
2 cloves garlic, crushed
1 teaspoon chili flakes
1 teaspoon ginger, grated
1 ½ (21-ounce) cans chickpeas (garbanzo beans), drained and rinsed
1 (14-ounce) can tomatoes
1 pound sweet potatoes, cut into bite-sized chunks
2 ¼ cups water
Salt and pepper

Preparation
1. Heat the coconut oil in a large, deep skillet over medium heat. Once the oil is shimmering, add the cumin seeds and fry until fragrant.
2. Add the onions with a pinch of salt and cook until soft and translucent, about 5 minutes. Throw in the garlic, chili flakes, and ginger and cook for another 5 minutes.
3. Pour the chickpeas, tomatoes, and sweet potatoes into the pan, together with 2 ¼ cups of water. Mix thoroughly.
4. Cover and simmer over low heat for about 30-40 minutes, or until the sweet potatoes become fork tender.

5. Taste and season the curry with salt and pepper. Serve piping hot.

Nutritional Facts (501 g per single serving)
Calories 373
Fats 13 g
Carbs 56 g
Protein 11 g
Sodium 522 mg

Coconut Butternut Squash Soup

Servings: 4

Ingredients
1 large butternut squash, about 1 ½ pounds
1 tablespoon coconut oil
1 onion, chopped
2 cups broth or water
2 tablespoons curry powder
2 teaspoons fresh ginger, grated
Pinch of ground nutmeg
1 (14-ounce) can light coconut milk
Salt and pepper

Preparation
1. Preheat the oven to 375°F. Line a shallow baking dish with aluminum foil.
2. Roast the whole squash for 20 minutes to soften the flesh slightly, to make it easier to cut through.
3. Take the squash out of the oven and cut it in half. Deseed it and place it cut-side down in the baking dish. Place the dish in the oven for another 40-50 minutes, or until a fork can easily pierce the flesh.
4. Once cooked, set the squash aside to let it cool for at least 20 minutes, then scoop the flesh out into a clean bowl.
5. Heat the coconut oil in a soup pot on medium-low heat. Sauté the onion until soft and translucent, about 5 minutes.
6. Add the squash, broth, curry powder, ginger, and nutmeg, and bring the mixture up to a boil before lowering the heat to low. Cover with a lid and allow it to simmer for 10 minutes.

7. Using an immersion blender, blend the soup until it becomes a smooth puree.
8. Pour in the coconut milk while stirring constantly, and heat through, about 5 minutes. Taste, and season with salt and pepper. Serve hot.

Nutritional Facts (427 g per single serving)
Calories 406
Fats 34 g
Carbs 27 g
Protein 4 g
Sodium 350 mg

Roasted Cauliflower with Lentils Salad

Servings: 4

Ingredients
1 head cauliflower, cut into 1-inch florets
¼ cup plus 1 tablespoon coconut oil, melted
¼ teaspoon ground cumin
¼ teaspoon ground cinnamon
Pinch of cayenne
2 cups plus 2 tablespoons water
1 cup green lentils, rinsed
2 tablespoons tahini
3 tablespoons lemon juice
1 teaspoon honey
½ cup roasted, unsalted almonds
½ red onion, sliced
4 cups salad leaves
Salt and pepper

Preparation
1. Preheat the oven to 425°F. In a large mixing bowl, coat the cauliflower with ¼ cup of coconut oil. Sprinkle it with the cumin, cinnamon, and cayenne, and season it generously with salt and pepper.
2. Place the florets on a large rimmed baking sheet and space them out evenly. Roast the vegetables in the oven for 20 minutes, stirring mid-way. When done, the cauliflower should be golden brown and fork tender.
3. While the cauliflower is baking, prepare the lentils. In a deep saucepan, boil 2 cups of water and add the lentils.

4. Reduce the heat to medium and continue simmering the lentils until they become tender, about 20 minutes. Drain the excess water.
5. In a large mixing bowl, combine the tahini, lemon juice, honey, 1 tablespoon of melted coconut oil and 2 tablespoons of water to make the dressing. Mix thoroughly before throwing in the lentils. Season the mixture with salt and pepper.
6. Chop the almonds into coarse chunks, and add them to the lentils together with the roasted cauliflower, onion, and salad leaves.
7. Give everything a good toss before serving it on a clean platter.

Nutritional Facts (428 g per single serving)
Calories 587
Fats 38 g
Carbs 48 g
Protein 21 g
Sodium 74 mg

Kale and Brussels Sprouts Stir-Fry Noodles

Servings: 2

Ingredients
3 ½ ounces soba or pasta noodles
4 ounces shredded curly kale
2 teaspoons coconut oil
2 tablespoons fresh ginger, peeled and thinly sliced
1 red pepper, deseeded and thinly sliced
2 cups Brussels sprouts, quartered
1 tablespoon soy sauce
2 tablespoons rice wine
1 lime, zest and juice
¼ cup plus 3 tablespoons water

Preparation
1. In a medium saucepan, bring some water to a boil and cook the noodles according to the package instructions. Drain and set the noodles aside.
2. Heat the coconut oil in a large skillet over medium-high heat. Add the kale and ¼ cup of water. Cover with a lid, and allow it to steam for 1-2 minutes until the kale softens slightly.
3. Add the ginger, red pepper, and Brussels sprouts. Fry until the sprouts soften.
4. Whisk the soy sauce, rice wine, lime zest and juice, and 3 tablespoons of water to make a sauce.
5. Return the noodles to the pan. Pour in the soy sauce mixture and toss everything together.

Nutritional Facts (356 g per single serving)
Calories 141
Fats 13 g
Carbs 19 g
Protein 141 g
Sodium 1056 mg

Fried Rice with Broccoli and Tofu

Servings: 3

Ingredients
1 head of broccoli, cut into 1-inch florets, stems peeled and diced
½ pound firm tofu, diced
2 tablespoons coconut oil, divided
2 eggs
1 tablespoon soy sauce
2 cloves garlic, minced
1 tablespoon ginger, minced
1 bunch scallion, chopped
1 tablespoon fish sauce
White pepper
3 cups cooked rice

Preparation
1. Cook the broccoli until just tender, and pat the diced tofu dry with a clean kitchen towel.
2. Whisk the eggs and soy sauce together in a small bowl.
3. Heat 1 tablespoon of coconut oil in a large skillet over medium-high heat. Add the tofu and cook for 4-5 minutes, until it turns a light brown color on all sides. Set it aside in a clean bowl.
4. Add the remaining oil to the skillet and stir-fry the garlic, ginger, and scallion for about 20-30 seconds, until fragrant. Throw the fish sauce, egg mixture, and rice into the skillet and make sure they are well combined. Season with white pepper. Return the tofu to the pan to heat it up for about 1 minute.
5. Remove from the heat and serve.

Nutritional Facts (348 g per single serving)
Calories 482
Fats 20 g
Carbs 52 g
Protein 25 g
Sodium 896 mg

Quinoa Tabbouleh Salad

Servings: 4

Ingredients
¼ cup coconut oil, divided
1 cup quinoa
2 cups water
1 large yellow onion, finely chopped
1 teaspoon ground cumin
1 tablespoon ground coriander
½ teaspoon red pepper flakes
1 ½ tablespoons tomato paste
4 tomatoes, seeded and diced
1 (15-ounce) can chickpeas, drained and rinsed
5 green onions, finely chopped
2 tablespoons fresh mint, finely chopped
1 ½ cups fresh flat-leaf parsley, chopped
2 tablespoons lemon juice
2 tablespoons pomegranate molasses
1 tablespoon extra virgin olive oil
Salt and pepper
1 avocado, thinly sliced, for garnish
1/3 cucumber, sliced, for garnish

Preparation
1. In a medium saucepan, heat 1 tablespoon of coconut oil over medium-high heat. Toast the quinoa in the oil, making sure to stir it frequently for 1-2 minutes, or until dry.
2. Pour water over the toasted quinoa and bring it to a boil. Once boiled, reduce the heat to low and allow the water to reduce, about 15 minutes. Turn the heat off. Use a fork to fluff the quinoa, cover the pot and allow it to sit for 5 minutes.

3. Heat the remaining coconut oil in a medium skillet over medium-high heat. Throw in the onions and cook until soft and translucent, about 5 minutes. Add the cumin, coriander, red pepper flakes and tomato paste to the onions. Stir for 3 minutes.
4. Combine the onion mixture with the quinoa thoroughly before incorporating the tomatoes, chickpeas, green onions, mint, parsley, lemon juice, pomegranate molasses, and olive oil. Season the salad with salt and pepper to taste.
5. Plate and garnish with slices of avocado and cucumber.

Nutritional Facts (514 g per single serving)
Calories 539
Fats 27 g
Carbs 64 g
Protein 14 g
Sodium 191 mg

Spinach Sweet Potato Salad with Coconut Lime Dressing

Servings: 4

Ingredients
For the salad:
4 sweet potatoes, cut into bite-sized chunks
2 tablespoons coconut oil, melted
Salt and pepper
Juice of 1 lime
1 red onion, sliced into thin rings
1 pound baby spinach
2 cups cherry tomatoes
1 cup sliced almonds, plus some for garnish
1 avocado, diced

For the dressing:
Zest and juice of 2 limes
2/3 (10-ounce) can coconut cream
4 teaspoons fish sauce
Salt and pepper

Preparation
1. Preheat the oven to 400°F, and line a baking pan with parchment paper.
2. In a large mixing bowl, combine the sweet potatoes with the coconut oil and season with salt and pepper.
3. Place the sweet potato chunks on the baking pan and roast for 30 minutes, or until tender, stirring halfway through. Allow them to cool before assembling the salad.

4. Meanwhile, squeeze the juice of 1 lime over the onion rings and let it sit.
5. Whisk together all the dressing ingredients, and season with salt and pepper to taste.
6. Put together the salad by combining the sweet potatoes, onion, baby spinach, cherry tomatoes, almonds, and dressing.
7. Plate the salad and top it off with diced avocado and more almond slices.

Nutritional Facts (535 g per single serving)
Calories 744
Fats 18 g
Carbs 54 g
Protein 18 g
Sodium 589 mg

Kale and Red Pepper Frittata

Servings: 4

Ingredients
1 tablespoon coconut oil
1/3 cup onion, diced
½ cup red pepper, diced
½ cup zucchini, diced
2 cups kale, chopped
8 large eggs
½ cup almond or coconut milk
Salt and pepper

Preparation
1. Preheat the oven to 350°F.
2. In a medium bowl, combine the eggs and milk together. Season generously with salt and pepper.
3. In an oven-safe skillet, melt a tablespoon of coconut oil over medium heat. Saute the onion, red pepper, and zucchini until soft and tender, about 5 minutes.
4. Stir in the kale and cover the pan with a lid to allow the kale to steam and wilt, about 5 minutes.
5. Pour the egg mixture into the skillet and cook until the edges start to brown, about 4 minutes.
6. Put the skillet into the oven and cook for 10-15 minutes, or until the frittata is set.

Nutritional Facts (187 g per single serving)
Calories 247
Fats 19 g
Carbs 5 g
Protein 2 g
Sodium 151 mg

Baked Sweet Potato Fries

Servings: 4-5

Ingredients
3 large sweet potatoes, sliced into 1-inch strips
¼ cup coconut oil, melted
1 teaspoon garlic powder
1 teaspoon dried thyme
1 teaspoon cayenne pepper
1 teaspoon dried oregano
Salt and pepper

Preparation
1. Preheat the oven to 400°F. Line a baking tray with parchment paper.
2. In a medium bowl, whisk the coconut oil and spices together. Add the sweet potatoes and toss to coat the sweet potatoes well. Season with salt and pepper.
3. Place the fries on the baking tray, making sure they do not touch each other. Bake for 25-30 minutes, turning the fries halfway through.

Nutritional Facts (221 g per single serving)
Calories 89
Fats 14 g
Carbs 21 g
Protein 2 g
Sodium 55 mg

Coconut Hummus Dip or Dressing

Servings: 4-5

Ingredients
½ cup coconut oil, melted, divided
1 (14-ounce) can chickpeas
2 cloves garlic
1/3 cup cilantro
¼ teaspoon lemon juice
1 tablespoon tahini
Salt and pepper
Carrot sticks (for dipping)
Cucumber sticks (for dipping)

Preparation
1. In a food processor, combine 2 tablespoons of coconut oil, the chickpeas, garlic, cilantro, lemon juice, and tahini.
2. While blending, drizzle coconut oil in until the mixture becomes a smooth paste. Season with salt and pepper to taste. Give it a few more pulses to combine everything together.
3. Serve the hummus with carrot and cucumber sticks.

Nutritional Facts (97 g per single serving)
Calories 356
Fats 31 g
Carbs 16 g
Protein 5 g
Sodium 158 mg

Side Dish Recipes

Honey-Coconut Glazed Carrots

Servings: 4

Ingredients
1 pound whole carrots, peeled and sliced 1 inch thick
2 tablespoons coconut oil
2 tablespoons honey
2 tablespoons fresh thyme

Preparation
1. Fill a large and deep saucepan with water and bring it to a boil. Put the carrots into the boiling water and cook for about 10-15 minutes, or until tender but firm.
2. Drain the carrots in colander.
3. Meanwhile, whisk together the coconut oil, honey, and thyme in a large bowl.
4. Toss the drained carrots with the honey oil mixture, making sure everything is well combined.

Nutritional Facts (132 g per single serving)
Calories 140
Fats 7 g
Carbs 20 g
Protein 1 g
Sodium 80 mg

Zesty Coconut Rice with Cilantro

Servings: 4

Ingredients
1 tablespoon coconut oil
1 cup white rice
1 (14-ounce) can light coconut milk
1 lime, zest and juice from half the lime
Salt

Preparation
1. Heat the coconut oil in a small saucepan over medium-high heat.
2. Fry the rice in the oil for about a minute, and then pour the coconut milk into the pan and stir to combine. Bring the mixture to a boil before reducing the heat to low.
3. Cover the pan and allow the rice to simmer for 30-35 minutes. Remove from the heat and let the rice steam in the residual heat for another 10 minutes.
4. Add the lime zest and juice and salt to taste. Using a fork, fluff the rice while mixing in all the seasonings.
5. Serve warm.

Nutritional Facts (179 g per single serving)
Calories 427
Fats 28 g
Carbs 42 g
Protein 6 g
Sodium 17 mg

Easy Garlic and Soy Stir-Fry Vegetables

Servings: 6

Ingredients
1 cup broccoli florets
2 cloves garlic, minced
1 tablespoon soy sauce
1 teaspoon sesame oil
2 tablespoons coconut oil
½ red onion, cut into chunks
4 carrots, peeled and sliced
1 red bell pepper, cut into chunks
2 zucchini, sliced
1 cup sugar snap peas

Preparation
1. Place the washed broccoli florets in a large bowl, cover it with plastic wrap and microwave it for 1 minute.
2. Meanwhile, whisk the garlic, soy sauce, and sesame oil together in a small bowl.
3. Heat the coconut oil in a large skillet over medium heat. Soften the onion, carrots, and bell pepper in the skillet for about 4 minutes, then stir in the zucchini, sugar snap peas, and broccoli.
4. Combine the garlic-soy mixture with the vegetables and stir-fry for 1 minute. Season with salt and pepper to taste, and serve immediately.

Nutritional Facts (149 g per single serving)
Calories 68
Fats 3 g
Carbs 8 g
Protein 2 g
Sodium 220 mg

Roasted Garlic and Rosemary Potato Wedges

Servings: 6

Ingredients
4 large baking potatoes, scrubbed
4 tablespoons coconut oil, melted
1 teaspoon fresh garlic, minced
1 teaspoon fresh rosemary, minced
Salt and pepper

Preparation
1. Preheat the oven to 400°F, and line a baking sheet with parchment paper.
2. Cut each of the potatoes into 6 wedges
3. In a medium bowl, whisk together the coconut oil, garlic, and rosemary, together with salt and pepper to taste.
4. Coat the potatoes thoroughly with the seasoning. Place the potatoes on the baking sheet in a single layer.
5. Bake them for 30-35 minutes. Halfway through, flip the wedges to the other side to brown.
6. Sprinkle with more salt, and serve warm.

Nutritional Facts (256 g per single serving)
Calories 271
Fats 9 g
Carbs 49 g
Protein 5 g
Sodium 15 mg

Cauliflower Fried Rice

Servings: 6

Ingredients
1 head cauliflower, stems removed
1 tablespoon coconut oil
½ cup onion, diced
1 clove garlic, minced
Salt and pepper

Preparation
1. Using a cheese grater, grate the cauliflower florets into a rice-like texture.
2. Heat the coconut oil in a medium skillet over medium heat.
3. Fry the onion and garlic until softened and translucent, about 5 minutes.
4. Add the cauliflower, and stir it together to combine. Cook for about 4 minutes.
5. Season with salt and pepper, and serve warm.

Nutritional Facts (152 g per single serving)
Calories 60
Fats 3 g
Carbs 8 g
Protein 3 g
Sodium 42 mg

Caramelized Onions and Mushroom Couscous

Servings: 2

Ingredients
5 ounces vegetable or chicken stock
5 ounces couscous
2 tablespoons coconut oil, divided
4 shallots, finely sliced
1 red onion, finely sliced
5 ounces mushrooms, halved
1 clove garlic, minced
Salt and pepper
Handful of fresh parsley, for garnish

Preparation
1. To cook the couscous, heat the stock up in a small saucepan. Once it is boiling, turn the heat off and add the couscous grains. Cover with a lid and set it aside.
2. In a small skillet, heat 1 tablespoon of coconut oil over medium heat. Add the shallots and onion, together with salt and pepper to taste. Cook for 8-10 minutes, until the onions begin to brown and are lightly caramelized.
3. In another medium skillet, heat 1 tablespoon of coconut oil over medium-high heat. Saute the mushrooms and garlic for 2-3 minutes.
4. Using a fork, fluff the couscous grains, and season to taste with salt and pepper.
5. Combine the onions and mushrooms with the couscous before serving. Garnish with parsley.

Nutritional Facts (268 g per single serving)
Calories 467
Fats 14 g
Carbs 72 g
Protein 13 g
Sodium 20 mg

Dessert Recipes

Coconut Oil Puffed Rice Treats

Servings: 20

Ingredients
4 tablespoons butter
4 tablespoons coconut oil
2 bags mini marshmallows
12-13 cups puffed rice such as Rice Krispies®
Toppings, such as chocolate chips, sprinkles, M&Ms®
Non-stick cooking spray

Preparation
1. Line a 9x13 baking pan with parchment paper and spray generously with non-stick cooking spray. Coat your spatula with non-stick cooking spray to prevent the marshmallow from sticking.
2. Melt the butter and coconut oil in a large saucepan.
3. Add the marshmallows and stir constantly until everything has melted.
4. Remove from the heat. Add the puffed rice and your favorite toppings, before mixing everything thoroughly.
5. Working quickly, tip the mixture into the prepared pan and spread it into an even layer.
6. Sprinkle more toppings if desired. Allow the mixture to cool for about 10-15 minutes before cutting into it.

Nutritional Facts (31 g per single serving)
Calories 139
Fats 6 g
Carbs 22 g
Protein 1 g
Sodium 92 mg

Dairy-Free Coconut Chocolate Truffles

Servings: 30

Ingredients
8 ounces dark chocolate (at least 70% cacao), chopped
¼ cup coconut oil
3 tablespoons water
1 teaspoon vanilla extract
Pinch of sea salt
Optional toppings: Cocoa powder, shredded coconut, chopped nuts

Preparation
1. Place an 8-inch baking pan in the freezer to chill.
2. In a medium saucepan, bring some water to a boil. Place a glass bowl on the pot over the boiling water.
3. Melt the chocolate in the bowl, together with the coconut oil and water, until smooth. Slowly stir in the vanilla and sea salt.
4. Pour the chocolate into the chilled baking dish and place it in the refrigerator until the mixture hardens slightly, about 2 hours.
5. Using an ice-cream scoop, create 30 balls of chocolate truffle. Transfer them to a parchment-lined baking sheet and refrigerate it for 10 more minutes.
6. Dip the truffles in your favorite toppings.

Nutritional Facts (11 g per single serving)
Calories 62
Fats 5 g
Carbs 3 g
Protein 1 g
Sodium 2 mg

Key Lime Pie

Makes: One 9-inch pie

Ingredients
For the crust
14 graham crackers
4 tablespoons coconut oil, melted
4 tablespoons unsalted butter, melted
1 tablespoon sugar
½ teaspoon salt

For the pie:
4 large egg yolks
1 (14-ounce) can sweetened condensed milk
2 teaspoons lime zest
¾ cup lime juice
Pinch of salt

Preparation
1. Preheat the oven to 325°F.
2. In a food processor, pulse the graham crackers, coconut oil, butter, sugar, and salt until it reaches the texture of wet sand.
3. Transfer the mixture to a 9-inch pie dish and press it evenly into the bottom and sides to form a pie crust.
4. Bake the crust until golden brown, about 12-15 minutes. Halfway through, rotate the dish inside the oven. Set the crust aside to let it cool.
5. Move on to the filling. In a large mixing bowl, combine the egg yolks and condensed milk. With an electric hand mixer, cream them together for about 5 minutes, or until pale and doubled in volume.

6. Beat in the lime zest, lime juice, and salt until well combined.
7. Pour the filling into the crust and transfer the pie to the oven. Bake for 15-20 minutes, or until the filling no longer jiggles and is puffed around the edges.
8. Remove the pie from oven and let it cool completely before refrigerating it. Best served chilled.

Nutritional Facts (968 g per pie)
Calories 3172
Fats 170 g
Carbs 364 g
Protein 58 g
Sodium 1091 mg

Coconut Oil Chocolate Chip Cookies

Servings: 12

Ingredients
2 ¼ cups all-purpose flour
1 teaspoon baking soda
Pinch salt
¾ cup coconut oil, melted
¾ cup light brown sugar
2/3 cup granulated sugar
2 large eggs
1 teaspoon vanilla extract
2 cups semisweet chocolate chips

Preparation
1. Preheat the oven to 375°F. Line two 9x13 baking sheets with parchment paper.
2. In a large bowl, whisk the flour, baking soda, and salt together.
3. Using an electric mixer, cream the coconut oil, brown sugar, and granulated sugar on medium-high speed until the mixture becomes light and fluffy, about 4 minutes.
4. Crack in the eggs one at a time and combine, then add the vanilla extract.
5. Lower the speed to medium and slowly incorporate the dry ingredients.
6. Using a spatula, fold in the chocolate chips.
7. Divide the dough into 12 portions. Roll them into balls and arrange on the baking sheets, leaving sufficient space for them to spread.
8. Bake the cookies for 12-15 minutes, or until they turn golden brown. Halfway through, rotate the baking sheet for even baking.

9. Remove the cookies from the oven and transfer them to a wire rack to cool completely.

Nutritional Facts (101 g per single serving)
Calories 459
Fats 23 g
Carbs 62 g
Protein 5 g
Sodium 14 mg

Fudgy Chocolate Coconut Brownie

Servings: 16

Ingredients
4 ounces bittersweet chocolate
1 cup coconut oil
1 cup granulated sugar
1 cup light brown sugar
3 large eggs plus 1 egg yolk
1 teaspoon vanilla extract
¾ cup all-purpose flour
1 cup unsweetened cocoa powder
½ teaspoon salt
½ teaspoon baking soda

Preparation
1. Preheat the oven to 350°F. Grease a 9-inch springform pan with some coconut oil.
2. Place the chocolate and coconut oil in a large microwave-safe bowl. Microwave it in 30-second intervals, stirring after each, until the chocolate is melted and smooth.
3. Combine the white sugar, brown sugar, vanilla, eggs, and yolk with the chocolate mixture.
4. In another bowl, whisk together the flour, cocoa powder, salt, and baking soda.
5. Pour the wet ingredients into the dry ingredients in 2 or 3 batches, making sure the batter is well-combined each time, but avoid over-mixing the batter.
6. Transfer the batter to the prepared pan and bake for about 35 minutes, or until a toothpick inserted in the center comes out clean.

7. Remove from the oven and let the brownies cool completely before cutting into them.

Nutritional Facts (83 g per single serving)
Calories 377
Fats 21 g
Carbs 48 g
Protein 4 g
Sodium 21 mg

Moist Carrot Cake

Servings: 8

Ingredients
For cake:
1 cup brown sugar
¾ cup coconut oil, melted
¼ cup plain Greek yogurt
3 large eggs
2 teaspoons vanilla extract
2 cups all-purpose flour
1 teaspoon baking soda
2 teaspoons ground cinnamon
¼ teaspoon ground nutmeg
½ teaspoon salt
2 cups carrots, finely grated
¾ cup walnut, chopped

For cream cheese frosting:
8 ounces cream cheese, softened
½ cup unsalted butter, softened
2 cups confectioners' sugar
2 tablespoons heavy cream
2 teaspoons vanilla extract

Preparation
1. Preheat the oven to 350°F. Grease a 9-inch springform pan with some coconut oil.
2. In a large mixing bowl, cream the brown sugar and oil together on medium speed using an electric mixer. Beat in the yogurt until fully combined.
3. Add the eggs, one at a time, incorporating the mixture well with each addition. Stir in the vanilla.

4. In another bowl, whisk together the flour, baking soda, cinnamon, nutmeg and salt. Combine the wet ingredients into the dry ingredients in 2 or 3 batches, taking care to not overmix the batter.
5. Gently fold in the carrots and walnuts. Pour the batter into the prepared pan.
6. Bake the cake for 30-40 minutes, or until a toothpick inserted in the center comes out clean.
7. While the cake is cooling, prepare the frosting. In a medium mixing bowl, combine the cream cheese and butter with the hand mixer on medium speed.
8. Add the powdered sugar and continue beating until thick. Pour in the heavy cream and vanilla extract and beat for another 2 minutes.
9. Once the cake is completely cooled, apply a generous layer of frosting all over the cake. Chill in the fridge for at least 1 hour before serving.

Nutritional Facts (204 g per single serving)
Calories 830
Fats 52 g
Carbs 80 g
Protein 11 g
Sodium 140 mg

Coconut Glazed Donuts

Servings: 12

Ingredients
3 ½ cups bread flour
1 tablespoon baking powder
½ teaspoon baking soda
1 teaspoon salt, divided
¼ teaspoon ground nutmeg
4 tablespoons unsalted butter, melted
½ cup sugar
2 teaspoons vanilla extract, divided
1 ¼ cups canned coconut milk, divided
1 egg
4 cups coconut oil, for frying
2 cups sweetened shredded coconut
2 cups confectioners' sugar

Preparation
1. Whisk the flour, baking powder, baking soda, ½ teaspoon salt, and nutmeg together in a medium bowl.
2. In another large mixing bowl, beat together the butter, sugar, 1 teaspoon of vanilla extract, 1 cup of coconut milk and the egg.
3. Add the dry ingredients in 3 or 4 batches to the wet ingredients, mixing until a soft and sticky dough is formed.
4. In a deep, large skillet, heat 4 cups of coconut oil until the frying thermometer reaches 370°F.
5. Meanwhile, scoop out ¼ cup of dough and form it into a loose ball. Press your thumb down into the middle of the ball to create the donut hole. Repeat the process with all the dough.

6. Using a slotted spoon, gently lower 2 or 3 donuts at a time into the heated oil. Do not overcrowd the pot, and this will lower the oil temperature.
7. Fry the donuts for about 3 minutes, flipping halfway, until they puff up and turn golden brown.
8. Using a slotted spoon, scoop the cooked donuts out of the oil and drain any excess oil on some paper towels. Transfer them to a wire rack to cool down completely.
9. Once all the donuts are fried, move on to make the topping.
10. In a medium skillet, toast the shredded coconut on medium heat, stirring constantly until it browns. Remove it from the heat, and set it aside on a clean plate.
11. In a medium bowl, combine the remaining ½ teaspoon salt, 1 teaspoon vanilla extract, ¼ cup coconut milk and the powdered sugar until the mixture is glossy and smooth.
12. Prepare a wire rack set on top of piece of parchment paper.
13. Dunk one side of each donut into the glaze and allow the excess to drip off before dipping it into the toasted coconut. Place the coated donuts onto the prepared wire rack and allow the glaze to set for at least 30 minutes.

Nutritional Facts (86 g per single serving)
Calories 1355
Fats 10 g
Carbs 61 g
Protein 5 g
Sodium 236 mg

Rich Coconut Lemon Bars

Servings: 9

Ingredients
1 cup coconut flour
½ cup sweetened coconut, shredded
¾ cup sugar, divided
1/3 cup coconut oil, melted
2 eggs
¼ cup lemon juice
2 tablespoons cornstarch

Preparation
1. Preheat the oven to 350°F. Line a 9-inch square baking pan with parchment paper.
2. To make the crust, combine the coconut flour, coconut, ¼ cup sugar, and the coconut oil in a medium bowl. Press the mixture evenly into the bottom of the prepared pan and bake for 10 minutes. Remove it from the oven and set it aside to cool down.
3. Using an electric or hand mixer, beat the eggs thoroughly before adding the lemon juice, the remaining ½ cup of sugar, and cornstarch.
4. Pour the wet ingredients onto the cooled crust, and put it back into the oven to bake for another 18-20 minutes, or until the top is set and does not jiggle.
5. Remove it from oven and allow it to cool completely before cutting it into servings.

Nutritional Facts (94 g per single serving)
Calories 384
Fats 17 g
Carbs 48 g
Protein 10 g
Sodium 119 mg

Chocolate Coconut Cupcakes

Servings: 12

Ingredients
For cupcakes:
1 cup full-fat coconut milk
¾ cup granulated sugar
1/3 cup coconut oil
1 teaspoon vanilla extract
1 ¼ cups all-purpose flour
1/3 cup cocoa powder, sifted
¾ teaspoon baking soda
½ teaspoon baking powder
¼ teaspoon salt

For frosting:
12 ounces coconut cream, chilled overnight
½ cup powdered sugar
½ cup shredded coconut

Preparation
1. Preheat the oven to 350°F. Prepare a cupcake tin with paper liners.
2. In a medium mixing bowl, mix the coconut milk, sugar, coconut oil, and vanilla together until well incorporated.
3. In a separate large bowl, whisk the flour, cocoa powder, baking soda, baking powder and salt together.
4. Pour the wet ingredients into the dry ingredients in 2 or 3 batches, making sure each time that it is properly incorporated, but do not overmix the ingredients.

5. Pour the batter into each liner, filling them 2/3 full. Place the cupcakes into the oven and bake for 20 minutes, or until a toothpick inserted in the center comes out clean.
6. Remove from the oven and transfer to a cooling rack to let them cool completely.
7. To make the frosting, chill a medium metal bowl in the freezer before use. When ready to frost, pour the coconut cream into the bowl and beat on high speed until it becomes smooth. Add the powdered sugar and beat until soft peaks form.
8. Using an offset spatula, frost the cupcakes with the prepared coconut cream and sprinkle with shredded coconut. Chill it in the fridge for at least 15-20 minutes for the frosting to set.

Nutritional Facts (76 g per single serving)
Calories 273
Fats 21 g
Carbs 22 g
Protein 2 g
Sodium 14 mg

No-bake Coconut Truffle Balls

Servings: 12

Ingredients
1 ¾ cups unsweetened shredded coconut, divided
2 teaspoons coconut oil, melted
3 tablespoons maple syrup
2 tablespoons unsweetened coconut milk
½ teaspoon vanilla extract
½ teaspoon ground cinnamon
Pinch of sea salt

Preparation
1. In a food processor, mix 1 cup of shredded coconut flakes with the coconut oil. Process until a thick paste is formed.
2. Drizzle in the maple syrup, coconut milk, vanilla extract, cinnamon, and salt until well combined.
3. Tip the coconut paste into a clean, medium-sized bowl. Combine ½ cup of shredded coconut with the paste.
4. Divide and roll the mixture into 12 balls, rolling it in the remaining shredded coconut.
5. Allow it to set in the fridge for at least an hour before digging in.

Nutritional Facts (19 g per single serving)
Calories 97
Fats 8 g
Carbs 6 g
Protein 1 g
Sodium 4 mg

Conclusion

Coconut oil has been touted as a 'miracle' or 'super' food due to its numerous health benefits, including its moisturising and anti-bacterial effects. This is certainly a far cry from the past, when the scientific community decried it for its high levels of saturated fats. Researchers have now found that the nature of the coconut oil's saturated fat is precisely what makes it healthy, because it consists of shorter-chain fatty acids as compared to other types of saturated fats found in lard and butter.

To enjoy these health benefits, we need to introduce coconut oil into our diets. The recipes in this cookbook have shown that coconut oil is a highly versatile cooking oil that could be used in a variety of ways from frying to baking. I hope these recipes inspire you to start stocking coconut oil in your kitchen pantry and put it to more creative uses that will be good for you, in body and mind.

Appendix - Cooking Conversion Charts

1. Volumes

US Fluid Oz.	US	US Dry Oz.	Metric Liquid ml
¼ oz.	2 tsp.	1 oz.	10 ml.
½ oz.	1 tbsp.	2 oz.	15 ml.
1 oz.	2 tbsp.	3 oz.	30 ml.
2 oz.	¼ cup	3½ oz.	60 ml.
4 oz.	½ cup	4 oz.	125 ml.
6 oz.	¾ cup	6 oz.	175 ml.
8 oz.	1 cup	8 oz.	250 ml.

Tsp.= teaspoon - tbsp.= tablespoon – oz.= ounce – ml.= millimeter

2. Oven Temperatures

Celsius (ºC)	Fahrenheit (ºF)
90	220
110	225
120	250
140	275
150	300
160	325
180	350
190	375
200	400
215	425
230	450
250	475
260	500

Rounded numbers to the nearest 5th

Printed in Great Britain
by Amazon